At the
Café

Paul Humphrey

Photography by Chris Fairclough

W
FRANKLIN WATTS
LONDON · SYDNEY

First published in 2005 by
Franklin Watts
96 Leonard Street
London EC2A 4XD

Franklin Watts Australia
Level 17/207 Kent Street
Sydney NSW 2000

WORCESTERSHIRE COUNTY COUNCIL	
077	
Bertrams	30.07.06
J647.95	£8.99

© 2005 Franklin Watts

ISBN 0 7496 6175 5 (hbk)
ISBN 0 7496 6187 9 (pbk)

Dewey classification number: 647.95

A CIP catalogue record for this book is available
from the British Library.

Planning and production by Discovery Books Limited
Editor: Rachel Tisdale
Designer: Ian Winton
Photography: Chris Fairclough
Series advisors: Diana Bentley MA and Dee Reid MA
Fellows of Oxford Brookes University

The author, packager and publisher would like to thank the
following people for their participation in this book: Archie,
Bryn and Lucy Auger; Alison, George and Gabrielle Price for
the use of The Country Restaurant.

Printed in China

Contents

4

Archie and his mum are going to a café.

Can we sit here?

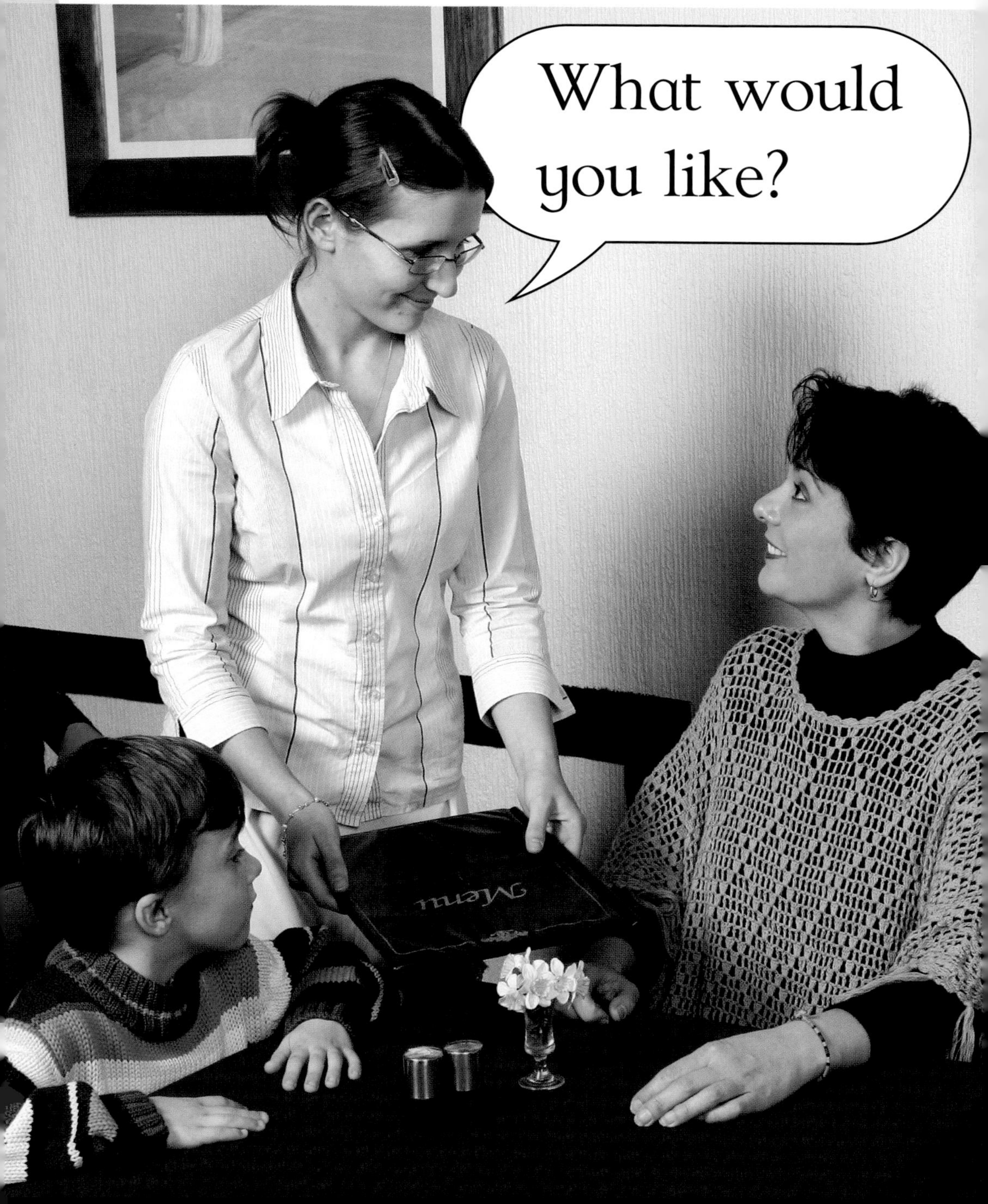
What would
you like?
Menu

MENU

<u>Drinks</u>

Tea..
Coffee.. 80p
Hot Chocolate.................................... £1.00
Fruit Juice (apple, orange, pineapple) £1.50
Milkshake.. 95p
Milk.. £1.10
Mineral Water.................................... 90p

<u>Cakes</u> £1.00

Toasted Tea Cake................................
Scone with butter............................... 95p
Scone with jam and cream.................. 90p
Gingerbread Man................................ £1.10
Danish Pastry..................................... £1.00
£1.10

Please can I have a gingerbread man?

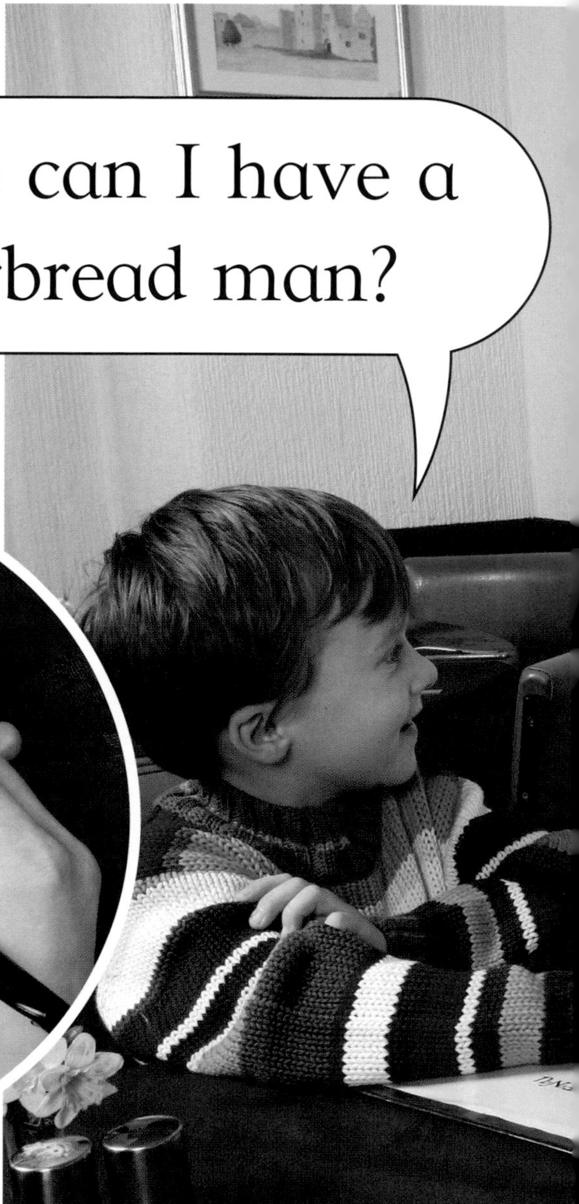

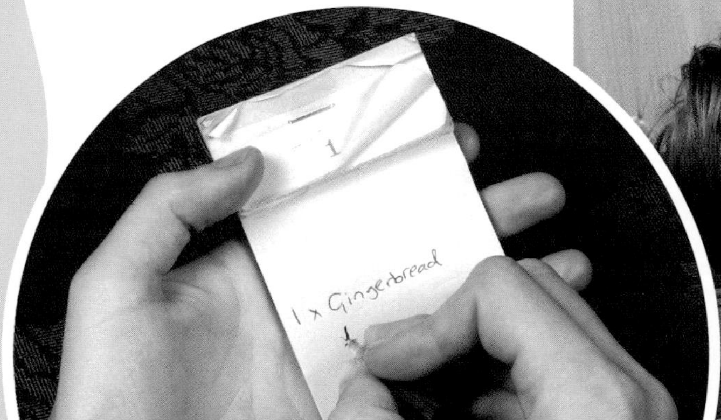

And I'd like a coffee, please.

First the waitress
chooses a
gingerbread man.

13

14

Then she pours the coffee.

She takes the tray to Archie and his mum.

Thank you.

17

Archie takes a bite of his gingerbread man.

19

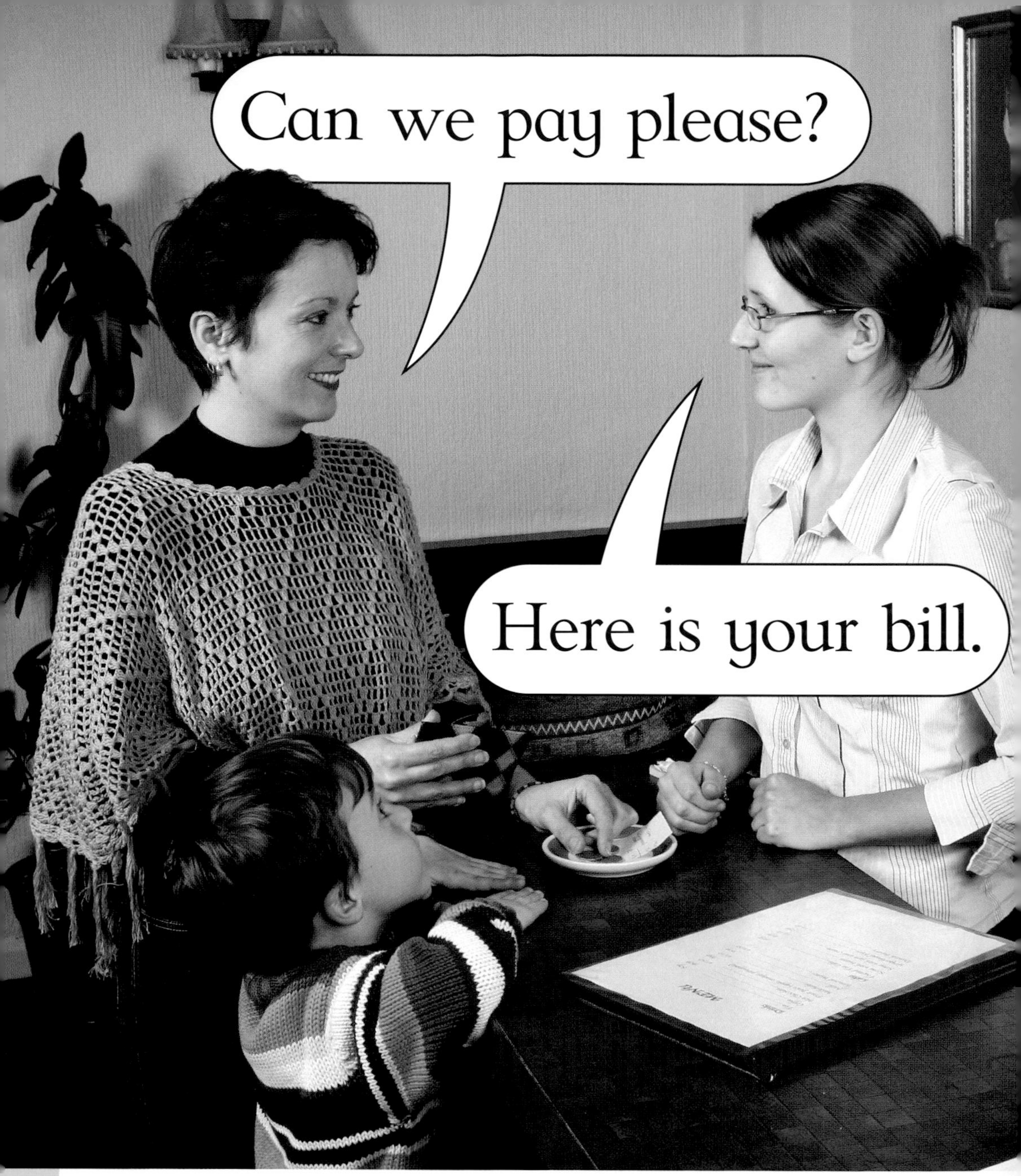
Can we pay please?
Here is your bill.

1 × Gingerbread £1·00
Man
1 × Coffee   £1·00
              ‾‾‾‾‾‾
              £2·00

ONLY CHILDREN
UP TO 12 YEARS
OF AGE ARE
PERMITTED TO
USE PLAY
EQUIPMENT

BY ORDER OF
TENBURY TOWN
COUNCIL

23

Word bank

Look back for these words and pictures.

Bill

Café

Coffee

Gingerbread man

Menu

Pay

Pours

Tray

Waitress